LaUnDEReD LiMERiCKs

FROM WICKED PENS

• • •

ILLUSTRATIONS BY
HENRY R. MARTIN

THE PETER PAUPER PRESS
MOUNT VERNON • NEW YORK

TO THE READER

Because new good limericks are prized but few are found, we are proud to offer the present collection. Most of these verses are new, and all, we hope, are good.

The reader should be warned that although many of these limericks are laundered and thus printable, there are many that are *still* not entirely clean. So please keep them away from children! We were tempted — now that four-letter words are being printed so freely — to include many a gay verse that depended on such words for their rhymes; but on the old-fashioned theory that a book should not read like a public comfort station, we have restrained ourselves. There are a few vulgarities here, but no obscenities. The book is thus somewhat purer than the average new novel.

The present collection is a sort of sequel to our *World's Best Limericks*, *Little Limerick Book*, and our larger volume, *Peter Pauper's Limerick Book*. The present limericks do not appear in any of these previous books.

We are indebted to a number of contributors who have sent us original verses and verses previously unknown to us. Heading the list is John Q. Anonymous, with many originals; others are

Robert S. Thompson	Carl F. Kauffeld
Julian E. Greenbaum	Don Kirchner
Bruce Angrave	W. D. Lewis
Seymour Berry	Frank Mittler
Thomas C. Chubb	W. A. Murdoch
Thomas Entz	Harry Pollak
Reva Freidberg	Arthur Rosenblum
Mary A. Harrington	O. H. K. Spate
H. M. Jalonack	

We thank these collaborators, and beg their indulgence for having in so many cases altered or rewritten their contributions.

A bather whose garments were strewed
On the beach where she sun-bathed all nude,
  Saw a man come along
  —And unless I'm quite wrong
You expected this line to be lewd.

A young couple quite fond of croquet
Were ready one morning to play;
   But the grass was all wet
    So they said: "Better yet,
Let us play other games in the hay."

• • •

A guy with a terrible cough
In winter time always would scough
   At warm woolen drawers
    When going outdawers —
Well, pneumonia carried him ough.

• • •

A fellow employed as a chauffeur
Decided one day that he'd gauffeur
   His rich boss' daughter;
    Thought he, if he caught her,
Thenceforth he could live as a lauffeur.

On a bus at the end of the day
Miss Fifi was prompted to say:
   "Please give me your seat,
   I'm dead on my feet:
I'm *enceinte* — or at least *fatiguée*."

     ●   ●   ●

A lassie from wee Ballachulish
Observed, "Och, virginity's foolish;
   When a lad makes a try
   To say aught but 'Aye'
Is stubborn, pig-headed, and mulish."

     ●   ●   ●

A young German farmer near Munich
One day wore a bright scarlet tunich,
   A bull took offense,
   And now this poor gent's
An unfortunate Teutonic unich.

There once was a fellow named Abbott
Who made love to girls as a habit;
    But he ran for the door
    When one girl asked for more,
And exclaimed "I'm a man, not a rabbit."

• • •

You probably never have heard
Of this rather eccentric old beard,
    Who lived in a hole
    In the ground, the poor sole,
To get used to being inteard.

• • •

When he looked at himself in a mirror,
A bird who'd been drunk for a yirror
    So said "Who's that guy?
    It couldn't be uy,"
But he kept feeling quirror and quirror.

A gorgeous voluptuous creature
Seduced a young Methodist preacher;
   It worked out quite well,
   For under his spell
This gal's now a Sunday-school teacher.

9

Said an eighty-year bridegroom named Carr,
"My libido's too high, Doc, by far;
   But it's all in my head,
   Move it down here instead,
For I'd still like to be a papa."

• • •

A sensitive lady from Worcester
At a ball met a fellow who gorcester;
   A lecherous guy
   With blood in his uy,
So she ducked out before he sedorcester.

• • •

An erudite author was Holmes,
Who wrote some most ponderous tomes,
   But somehow we feel
   That their only appeal
Is to folks with protuberant domes.

10

A Korean whose home was in Seoul
Had notions uncommonly droll;
   He'd get himself stewed
   And pose in the nude
On top of a telephone pole.

• • •

A stingy old girl up in Gloucester
Complained of what everything coucester;
   She'd go to the store,
   And the way she would rore
At the prices would almost exoucester.

• • •

Anon., Idem, Ibid, and Trad.
Wrote much that is morally bad:
   Some ballads, most chanteys,
   All poems on panties —
And limericks too, one must add.

There was a young lady named Frances
Who suffered embarrassing trances;
    She stripped to the skin
    Before Father O'Flynn
And made him indecent advances.

• • •

There was an old lecher named Gus
Who wore a horrible truss;
    It would pinch, sweat and itch,
    When the son of a bitch
Got too close to young girls on a bus.

• • •

A herder who hailed from Terre Haute
Fell in love with a young nanny goat;
    The daughter he sired
    Was greatly admired
For her beautiful angora coat.

A naked young tart named Roselle
Walked the streets while ringing a bell;
   When asked why she rang it
   She answered, "Gol dang it!
Can't you see I have something to sell?"

The limerick's an art form complex
Whose contents run chiefly to sex;
   It's famous for virgins
   And masculine urgin's,
And vulgar erotic effects.

●   ●   ●

In merchandise Macy's a symbol
For anything down to a thymbol;
   But there is no doubt
   That if they are oubt,
You'll be able to get it from Gymbol.

●   ●   ●

A gal rather husky of limb
And waist took a course at a gimb
   To help her reduce,
   But it wasn't much use —
She still hasn't got her a himb.

14

Though his actions and motives were pure,
His friends became fure and fure;
  Then one day it occurred
  To this ostracized burred
'Twas because he worked down in a sure.

●   ●   ●

An adventurous fun-loving polyp
Propositioned a cute little scallop
  Down under the sea;
  "Nothing doing," said she,
"By Triton, do you think I'm a trollop?"

●   ●   ●

There once was a girl from Adair
Whose rump was all covered with hair;
  When her beau dropped her drawers
  He exclaimed with applause,
"You're lovely! You look like my mare!"

There was a young laundress named Singer
Whose bust was a round pink humdinger;
   But flat, black and blue
   It emerged into view
The day it got caught in the wringer.

●   ●   ●

Said the Bishop one day to the Abbott,
Whose instincts were just like a rabbit:
   "I know it's great fun
   To embrace a young nun —
But you mustn't get into the habit.

●   ●   ●

A venturesome three-weeks-old Chamois
Strayed off in the woods from his mamois
   And might have been dead,
   But some picnickers fed
Him with sandwiches, milk, and salamois.

A bashful Arabian Sheik
Had a nature entirely unique;
    At sight of a frail
    He'd turn deathly pale,
And hide in his tent for a week.

●   ●   ●

A violent girl from Anjou
Found necking affected her hue:
    She presented to sight
    Some parts pink and white
And others quite purple and blue.

●   ●   ●

An effeminate fellow from Lincoln
One night did some serious drincoln,
    Met a gal, now his wife,
    Learned the real facts of life,
And blesses the day he got stincoln.

There was a young fellow of Dee
Made love to an ape in a tree;
    The result was quite horrid:
    All chin and no forehead,
Green teeth, and a purple goatee.

• • •

There once was an elderly Cree
Who was mad about whisky in tea;
    He drank ninety-five cups,
    Gave a couple of brrups,
And died in his own warm tepee.

• • •

There was a fat rabbit in Surrey
Who ran down the lane in a hurry;
    He remarked: "I'm pursued,
    And by God I'll be stewed
If I'm caught, and eaten with curry."

Said the Duke to the Duchess of Avery,
"Forgive me for breaking your reverie;
   You've been sitting on *Punch*
   Since long before lunch —
Might I have it, before it's unsavory?"

● ● ●

Said a cellist, a modest young fellow,
When praised for playing so mellow:
   "It's the easiest thing:
   I just butter each string
With a *soupçon* of strawberry jello."

● ● ●

A merchant addressing a debtor
Remarked in the course of his lebtor
   That he chose to suppose
   A man knose what he ose
And the sooner he pays it the bebtor.

There was a young man from Montrose
Who had a triangular nose;
    The cube of its weight
    Plus his sinus times eight
Equaled two-thirds of three-fourths of his toes.

•   •   •

An eccentric old spinster named Lowell
Announced to her friends, "Bless my sowell,
    I've gained so much weight
    I am sorry to state
I fear that I'm going to fowell."

•   •   •

An unfortunate maiden was Esther,
A peculiar repugnance possessed her;
    A reaction compulsive
    Made kissing repulsive,
Which was rough on all those who caressed her.

One night a young amorous Sioux
Had a date with a maiden he knioux;
    The coroner found
    The couple had drowned
Making love in a leaky canioux.

To Sadie the touch of a male meant
An emotional cardiac ailment;
    And acute shortness of breath
    Caused her untimely death
In the course of erotic impalement.

● ● ●

There was a young lady of Zion
Looked round for a shoulder to cry on;
    So she married a spouse
    From a very old house
And started to cry on the scion.

● ● ●

A lady who lived in Caracas
Was wed to a silly old jackass;
    When he started to cheat her
    With a gay senorita
She raised a most violent fracas.

There was a young girl from St. Paul
Who went to a birth-control ball
   With high expectations
   To give demonstrations,
But nobody asked her at all.

      •   •   •

An unfortunate lad from Calcutta
Vibrated all through like a stutter;
   To eat, walk or speak
   He would shake for a week,
But he *was* rather good as a rutter.

      •   •   •

The bashful young bachelor Cleary
Of girls was exceedingly leery;
   Then a lady named Lou
   Showed him how and with who
He could render his evenings more cheery.

"I wouldn't be bothered with drawers,"
Says one of our better-known whawers;
  "There isn't much doubt
  I do better withoubt
In handling my everyday chawers."

●　　●　　●

In a lovely young girl from Mungoes
An unfortunate habit arose:
  When having a tete-
  a-tete with a date,
She'd spend the time picking her nose.

●　　●　　●

There was a young fellow named Pete
Who was gentle, and shy, and discreet;
  But with his first woman
  He became quite inhuman
And constantly roared for fresh meat.

A God-fearing maiden from Goshen
Took a September-Morn swim in the ocean;
   When a whirlpool appeared
   She rose up and cheered,
And developed a rotary motion.

There was a young maiden named Hoople
Whose bosom was triple, not douple;
    So she had one removed
    But it grew back improved
And at present her front is quadruple.

•   •   •

There was a young man with a hernia,
Who said to his surgeon, "Gol dern ya,
    Now don't make a botch
    Of this job on my crotch,
Or cut things that do not concern ya."

•   •   •

In Wall Street a girl named Irene
Made an offering somewhat obscene:
    She stripped herself bare
    And offered a share
To Merrill, Lynch, Pierce, Fenner, Smith
    and Beane.

A holy young cow of Calcutta
Confided one day to her brudder
    That when she goes swimmin'
    With other young women
She steers by the use of her udder.

    ● ● ●

There was a young fellow named Hill
Who took a uranium pill;
    His entrails corroded,
    His belly exploded,
And his eyeballs were found in Brazil.

    ● ● ●

That flatulent burper McGee
Was gassy as humans can be;
    He delighted his friends
    With duets from both ends,
But he goofed on "Oh Promise Me!"

"Gracious me," said the Duke of Buccleugh,
"I've been struck from the rolls of *Who's Who!*
　　All because I was seen
　　Making love on the green
With my granny, and very nice too!"

·　·　·

There was an old spinster of Worcester
Who owned nine grey hens and a rooster;
　　When the rooster expired
　　She often inquired
Why there weren't new chicks like there uster.

·　·　·

An agreeable man from Jerusalem
From a Christian turned into a Muzzelim;
　　And later he too
　　Turned into a Jew:
And remarked, "That surely will puzzle 'em!"

A luscious young damsel named Florence
Fell into the frigid St. Lawrence,
    Where poor famished fish
    Made this beautiful dish
An object of utter abhorrence.

A baritone star from Havana
Slipped horribly on a banana;
 He was sick for a year
 Then resumed his career
As a promising lyric soprana.

• • •

There is a young lady named Aird
Whose bottom is always kept bared;
 When asked why, she pouts,
 And says the Boy Scouts
All beg her to *please* Be Prepared.

• • •

There was a fat lady from Eye
Who felt she was likely to die;
 But for fear that once dead
 She would not be well-fed,
She gulped down a pig, a cow, a sheep,
 twelve buns, a seven-layer cake, four
 cups of coffee, and a green-apple pie.

There was a young farmer named Max
Who avoided the gasoline tax;
    It was simple, you see,
    For his Vespa burned pee
From his grandfather's herd of tame yaks.

        ●   ●   ●

A husband who lived in Tiberias,
Once laughed himself nearly delirious;
    But he laughed at his wife
    Who took a sharp knife
With results that were quite deleterious.

        ●   ●   ●

There was a young fellow named Reed
Who had an emotional need;
    So to shock his best friends
    He went to great ends:
He stood on his head when he peed.

A guy with a girl in a Fiat
Asked, "Where on earth is my key at?"
   When he started to seek
   She let out with a shriek
"That's *not* where it's likely to be at!"

· · ·

A senile decrepit crustacean
His mind on a mild molestation,
   Attempted to grab
   A curvaceous young crab,
But experienced only frustration.

· · ·

A bather in Lake Ballyclear
Had a front that would burst a brassiere;
   She had a round face
   And was plump every place
Except for a flat-chested rear.

They sat in his little old Lloyd
Frustrated, and hot, and annoyed;
    But enough of palaver:
    He attempted to have 'er
And the car was entirely destroyed.

      ●   ●   ●

While trying to live like a Bedouin,
A thrill-hunting fellow named Edouin
    Attempted to sneak
    A cute slave from a Sheik,
And in no time at all was a dedouin.

      ●   ●   ●

There was a young fellow in Maine
Who courted a girl all in vain;
    She cussed when he kissed her
    So he slept with her sister
Again and again and again!

If intercourse gives you thrombosis
While continence causes neurosis,
   I prefer to expire
   Fulfilling desire
Than live on in a state of psychosis.

• • •

There was a young fellow named Abel
Whose mind was a trifle unstable;
   When ladies gave teas,
   On his hands and his knees
He'd go feeling the legs of each table.

• • •

There once was a bulldog named Caesar,
Saw a cat and decided to taesar;
   But she scratched and she spit
   Till the big bulldog quit:
Now Caesar just saesar and flaesar.

There was an old maid of Peru
Who thirty-one languages knew;
   With one pair of lungs
   She worked thirty-one tongues,
But choked when she tried thirty-two.

     ●   ●   ●

There was a young lady named Gay
Who was asked to make love in the hay;
   She jumped at the chance
   And took off her pants:
She was tickled to try it that way.

     ●   ●   ●

There was a young woman named Sue
Who saw a strange beast in the zoo;
   When she asked, "Is it old?"
   She firmly was told,
"No! Certainly not! It is gnu."

There once was a fellow named Brett
Loved a girl in his shiny Corvette;
    We know it's absurd
    But the last that we heard
They hadn't untangled them yet.

● ● ●

A man who was crude and uncouth
Met up with a maiden named Ruth;
    But she gave him the air
    When he tried to betray 'er
One night in a telephone booth.

● ● ●

A plumber from Lowater Creek
Was called in by a dame with a leak;
    She looked so becoming
    He fixed *all* her plumbing
And didn't emerge for a week.

A buxom young beauty named Beulah
Each night entertained with a hula;
   'Twas rather *risqué*
   In a mild sort of way,
But she made quite a bundle of moula.

A forward young fellow named Tarr
Had a habit of goosing his Ma;
   "Go pester your sister,"
   She said when he kissed her,
"I've trouble enough with your Pa."

●   ●   ●

That talkative gourmand, old Gutter,
Had a violent kind of a stutter;
   His merry glass eye
   Often popped in the pie,
And his teeth jumped into the butter.

●   ●   ●

A flatulent fellow named Snite
Was so full of gas he was tight;
   He blended with art
   His belch and his fart,
But the timing was never quite right.

A Boston co-ed nicknamed Snooks
Whose pleasure till then had been books,
    Once caught her a Cabot
    Who looked like a rabbit
And really loved up to his looks.

      ●   ●   ●

There was a young parson named Bings,
Who talked about God and such things;
    But his secret desire
    Was a maid in the choir,
With a bottom like jelly on springs.

      ●   ●   ●

There was a young lady of Pecking
Who indulged in a great deal of necking;
    This seemed a great waste
    Since she claimed to be chaste:
This statement, however, needs checking.

In Summer he said she was fair,
In Autumn her charms were still there;
    But he said to his wife
    In the Winter of life
"There's no Spring in your old *derrière*."

•   •   •

A senile old lecher named Spratt
Once went on a terrible bat;
    If a girl weren't alert
    He'd reach under her skirt
And claim to be petting a cat.

•   •   •

A hapless church tenor was Horace,
Whose skin was so terribly porous,
    Sometimes in the choir
    He'd start to perspire,
And damn nearly drown out the chorus.

A minister up in Vermont
Keeps a goldfish alive in the font;
   When he dips the babes in,
   It tickles their skin,
Which is all that the innocents want.

A brainy professor named Zed
Dreamed one night of a buxom co-ed;
   He mussed her and bussed her
   And otherwise fussed her,
But the action was all in his head.

● ● ●

A well-behaved creature, the oyster
Cares not to carouse or to royster;
   He never gets high,
   But his life isn't drigh —
In fact it could hardly be moyster.

● ● ●

A remarkable feature has Myrtle,
A retractable neck like a turtle;
   But though she has never
   Been called handsome or clever
She annually proves to be fertile.

A lady removing her scanties
Heard them crackle electrical chanteys;
   Said her husband, "My dear,
   I very much fear
You suffer from amps in your panties."

● ● ●

There was a young man from Montrose
Who could tickle himself with his toes;
   The trick was so neat,
   He fell in love with his feet,
And christened them Myrtle and Rose.

● ● ●

The Reverend Mr. Uprightly
Was cuckolded daily and nightly;
   He murmured "Dear, dear!
   I would fain interfere,
If I knew how to do it politely."

A jocular fellow from Ghent
Once remarked to his wife, quite *enceinte;*
   "I like your new dress,
   But don't you think, Bess,
You'd more easily fit in a tent?"

     ●   ●   ●

At a banquet once in Ballockery,
The waiters were dropping the crockery;
   Said one guest in despair
   Combing peas from his hair:
"This isn't a meal, it's a mockery."

     ●   ●   ●

There was a young girl from Mobile
Whose crotch was made of blue steel;
   She got all her thrills
   From pneumatic drills,
And an off-center emery wheel.

There was a young fellow named Willy
Who acted remarkably silly:
  At an All-Nations ball
  Dressed in nothing at all
He swore that his costume was Chile.

Sighed an Englishman, after a dance,
When a lady had called him a nance,
   "Though my first name is Cyril,
   My instincts are virile," —
And he suddenly pulled down his pants.

●   ●   ●

There was a young lady from Brussels
Who was proud of her *derrière* muscles;
   She could easily plex them,
   And so interflex them,
As to whistle a tune through her bustles.

●   ●   ●

"It's my habit," said sweet Lady Norris,
"To ask lifts from the drivers of lorries;
   And I thus get much play
   Unsuited, I'd say,
To the seat of my miniscule Morris."

46

A remarkable race are the Persians,
They have such peculiar diversions;
    They make love all the day
    In the regular way
And all night they practice perversions.

    ●   ●   ●

There was a young maiden named Nellie
Whose breasts could be joggled like jelly;
    They could tie in a knot
    Or reach you-know-what,
Or even swat flies on her belly.

    ●   ●   ●

A perverted young lad from Bengal
Once went to a fancy-dress ball
    Arrayed like a tree:
    But he failed to foresee
That the dogs wouldn't use him at all.

An orthodox Jewess with joy
Gave birth to a fine baby boy;
    But her husband, the fool,
    When he saw the child's tool,
Remarked, "Oh my God, it's a *goy!*"

      ●   ●   ●

"My girl-friend wants me to ski,"
Said the flabby young cellist, "but Gee!
    With Stravinsky, Stokowski,
    Mussorghsky, Tchaikowsky,
That's quite enough skiing for me."

      ●   ●   ●

An orchestra leader named Prime
Had devotion to art quite sublime:
    For always he'd pee
    To "O say can you see!"
And he'd wave his baton to keep time.

An obnoxious young man from the Oxus
Said: "How strong the smell of my sox is";
    So holding his nose
    He pulled off his hose
And put the offenders in boxes.

An ardent disciple of Freud
Lost out with a lady named Lleud;
   She was far from a prude,
   But this lad was imbued
With urges that shocked and anneud.

• • •

There was a young man of high station,
Who was found by a pious relation
   Making love on the floor,
   To — I won't say a hoor,
But a lady of poor reputation.

• • •

A critic refused, as reviewer,
To read the obscene and impure;
   He soon left the scene,
   For the books that were clean
Just kept getting fewer and fewer.

A visitor once to Loch Ness
Met the monster, who left him a mess;
   They returned his entrails
   By the regular mails,
And the rest of the stuff by express.

● ● ●

There was a young girl of Dumfries
Who said to her beau, "If you please,
   It would give me great bliss,
   If, while playing with this,
You would pay some attention to these."

● ● ●

A gentle old dame they called Muir,
Had a mind so delightfully pure
   That she fainted away
   At a friend's house one day,
When she saw some canary manure.

51

A hermit once thought his oasis
The best of all possible places:
   For it had a mirage
   In the form of a large
And affectionate female curvaceous.

● ● ●

An amorous maiden antique
Locked a man in her house for a week;
   He entered her door
   With a shout and a roar,
But his exit was marked by a squeak.

● ● ●

A lad who loved all that was lewd,
And the better emotions eschewed,
   By one of fate's quirks
   Gummed up his own works —
He married a regular prude.

There was a young lady named Carol
Played two-handed stud for apparel;
   Her opponent's straight flush
   Brought a maidenly blush,
And a hasty trip home in a barrel.

There was a young lady named Gloria
Who was goosed by Sir Oswald Du Maurier,
   And then by six men,
   Sir Oswald again,
And the band at the Waldorf-Astoria.

• • •

There was a young girl from West Chester
Whose sweetheart kissed and caressed her;
   But she said that his throes
   Would ruin her clothes,
And so he completely undressed her.

• • •

A fellow who lived on the Isthmus
Of Suez was cursed with strabismus;
   He couldn't see straight
   When he looked at the date,
And thought Easter Sunday was Christmas.

A fox-hunting lady named Maud
At love was a terrible fraud;
    With the boys in the stable
    She was willing and able,
But in bed with her spouse she was bored.

       •   •   •

There was a young lady from Devon
Who was goosed in the garden by seven
    High Anglican priests
    (The lascivious beasts!) —
Of such is the Kingdom of Heaven!

       •   •   •

A dame who seemed statuesque
Once stripped at the local burlesque;
    Her breasts were stupendous
    Her bottom horrendous —
But her navel was almost grotesque.

A team playing baseball in Dallas
Called the umpire "Crook!" out of malice;
    While this worthy had fits,
    The team made eight hits
And a girl in the bleachers named Alice.

● ● ●

There was a young woman named Bunny
Whose kisses were sweeter than honey;
    And male callers galore
    Would line up at her door,
To take turns in paying her money.

● ● ●

The Model-T Ford of old Jake's
Has the miseries, megrims and shakes:
    Like a pneumatic drill
    It can never stand still,
But hiccups, and chatters its brakes.

An old maid in the land of Aloha
Got wrapped in the coils of a boa;
  And as the snake squeezed
  The maid, not displeased,
Cried, "Darling! I love it! Samoa!"

There was a young fellow from Clyde
Who fell down an outhouse and died;
   His unfortunate brother
   Then fell down another,
And now they're interred side by side.

     ●   ●   ●

An ambitious young amateur sleuth
Behaved in a manner uncouth;
   In pursuing a victim,
   He floored him and kicked him,
And fractured his features forsooth.

     ●   ●   ●

There was a young lady named Etta
Who fancied herself in a sweater;
   Three reasons she had:
   To keep warm was not bad,
But the other two reasons were better.

A fellow from old Copenhagen
Wooed a girl in his little Volkswagen;
   But the damage was high:
   The stick-shift in his eye,
And a gash from the dash on his noggin.

      •   •   •

Despite her impressive physique
Fatima was really quite meek;
   If a mouse showed its head,
   She would jump into bed
With a terrible blood-curdling sheik.

      •   •   •

Said a man of his small Morris Minor
"For petting, it couldn't be finer;
   But for love's consummation
   A wagon called station
Would offer a playground diviner."

There was a young girl from Grant's Pass
Who loved to tickle her ass;
    Her favorite trick
    Was to use a sharp stick
And scratch it while feeding it grass.